EMMANUEL JOSEPH

Empowered Silence: Harnessing the Power of Quietude

Copyright © 2025 by Emmanuel Joseph

All rights reserved. No part of this publication may be reproduced, stored or transmitted in any form or by any means, electronic, mechanical, photocopying, recording, scanning, or otherwise without written permission from the publisher. It is illegal to copy this book, post it to a website, or distribute it by any other means without permission.

First edition

This book was professionally typeset on Reedsy. Find out more at reedsy.com

Contents

1. Chapter 1: The Essence of Silence — 1
2. Chapter 2: The Science Behind Silence — 2
3. Chapter 3: Silence in Nature — 3
4. Chapter 4: The Role of Silence in Relationships — 4
5. Chapter 5: Silence as a Path to Self-Discovery — 5
6. Chapter 6: The Art of Mindful Silence — 6
7. Chapter 7: Silence in the Workplace — 7
8. Chapter 8: The Spiritual Dimension of Silence — 8
9. Chapter 9: Cultivating Silence in Daily Life — 9
10. Chapter 10: Overcoming the Fear of Silence — 10
11. Chapter 11: Silence as a Catalyst for Creativity — 12
12. Chapter 12: Embracing Silence for a Balanced Life — 13
13. Chapter 13: Silence in Cultural Traditions — 14
14. Chapter 14: The Healing Power of Silence — 15
15. Chapter 15: Silence and Mental Clarity — 16
16. Chapter 16: Creating a Personal Silence Sanctuary — 17
17. Chapter 17: Silence and the Art of Listening — 18

1

Chapter 1: The Essence of Silence

In today's fast-paced world, the idea of silence can be both alluring and intimidating. Silence, often perceived as emptiness or absence, is in fact a powerful state that holds the potential for profound clarity and inner peace. It's in these quiet moments that we can truly connect with ourselves and the world around us.

Embracing silence requires a shift in perspective. Rather than viewing it as a void, we can see it as a space filled with potential. Silence allows our minds to wander freely, fostering creativity and innovation. It is in these silent interludes that our best ideas often emerge.

Moreover, silence provides a break from the constant barrage of stimuli we encounter daily. It offers a respite for our senses and a chance for our minds to rest and rejuvenate. In the quiet, we find an opportunity to reflect, to process our experiences, and to gain a deeper understanding of our emotions.

Ultimately, silence is a powerful tool for personal growth. It is in these quiet moments that we can confront our innermost thoughts and feelings, leading to greater self-awareness and emotional resilience. By embracing silence, we unlock the potential for profound personal transformation.

2

Chapter 2: The Science Behind Silence

Scientific research has shown that silence has a significant impact on our mental and physical well-being. Studies have demonstrated that silence can reduce stress, lower blood pressure, and improve cognitive function. These findings underscore the importance of incorporating moments of quiet into our daily lives.

One of the key ways silence benefits our brain is through the process of neurogenesis, the creation of new neurons. Silence has been found to stimulate the growth of new brain cells in the hippocampus, the region of the brain associated with memory, emotion, and learning. This highlights the role of silence in enhancing our cognitive abilities.

Furthermore, silence has been shown to activate the brain's default mode network (DMN). The DMN is responsible for introspective activities such as daydreaming, self-reflection, and future planning. When we engage in silent contemplation, we allow our DMN to function optimally, fostering creativity and problem-solving.

In addition to its cognitive benefits, silence also promotes emotional well-being. It provides a space for us to process our emotions and experiences, leading to greater emotional clarity and stability. By embracing silence, we create an environment in which our minds can heal and flourish.

3

Chapter 3: Silence in Nature

Nature offers some of the most profound experiences of silence. The stillness of a forest, the tranquility of a secluded beach, or the quiet of a mountain peak can evoke a deep sense of peace and connection. These natural environments provide an ideal setting for embracing the power of silence.

Spending time in nature allows us to escape the noise and distractions of modern life. In these quiet settings, we can fully immerse ourselves in the present moment, attuning our senses to the subtle sounds of the natural world. This heightened awareness fosters a sense of mindfulness and appreciation for the beauty around us.

Moreover, nature's silence has a calming effect on our nervous system. The soothing sounds of rustling leaves, flowing water, or birdsong can reduce stress and anxiety, promoting a sense of relaxation and well-being. These natural soundscapes offer a gentle reminder of the restorative power of silence.

By seeking out moments of silence in nature, we can cultivate a deeper connection with the world around us. This connection fosters a sense of belonging and grounding, reminding us of our place within the larger tapestry of life. Nature's silence is a powerful catalyst for inner peace and personal growth.

4

Chapter 4: The Role of Silence in Relationships

Silence plays a crucial role in our relationships with others. While communication is often seen as the cornerstone of strong relationships, silence can be equally important. It is in these quiet moments that we can truly listen, understand, and connect with those around us.

Active listening is a vital skill that requires us to be fully present and attentive. By embracing silence, we create a space for others to express themselves without interruption. This fosters deeper understanding and empathy, strengthening our connections with others.

Furthermore, silence can be a powerful tool for conflict resolution. In moments of tension or disagreement, taking a step back and allowing for a period of silence can provide the necessary space for reflection and perspective. This can lead to more thoughtful and constructive communication.

In addition to its role in conflict resolution, silence also enhances the quality of our interactions. Moments of shared silence can create a sense of intimacy and trust, fostering deeper emotional bonds. By valuing and embracing silence, we enrich our relationships and cultivate meaningful connections.

5

Chapter 5: Silence as a Path to Self-Discovery

Silence offers a unique opportunity for self-discovery. In the absence of external noise and distractions, we can turn our attention inward and explore our inner landscape. This journey of self-reflection can lead to greater self-awareness and personal growth.

Engaging in regular periods of silence allows us to reconnect with our true selves. It provides a space for introspection, enabling us to identify our values, passions, and aspirations. Through this process, we gain a clearer understanding of who we are and what we want in life.

Moreover, silence encourages us to confront our innermost thoughts and feelings. This can be a challenging but ultimately rewarding experience, as it allows us to address unresolved issues and gain insight into our emotional patterns. By embracing silence, we cultivate emotional resilience and inner strength.

Ultimately, silence is a powerful tool for self-discovery and personal transformation. It is in these quiet moments that we can gain clarity, set intentions, and align our actions with our true selves. By harnessing the power of silence, we embark on a journey of self-discovery and growth.

6

Chapter 6: The Art of Mindful Silence

Mindfulness is the practice of being fully present and engaged in the moment. When combined with silence, mindfulness becomes a powerful tool for enhancing our awareness and deepening our connection with ourselves and the world around us.

Practicing mindful silence involves intentionally creating moments of quiet in our daily lives. This can be as simple as taking a few minutes each day to sit in silence, focusing on our breath, or engaging in a silent walk in nature. These practices help us cultivate a sense of calm and clarity.

In mindful silence, we learn to observe our thoughts and emotions without judgment. This heightened awareness allows us to respond to situations with greater intention and wisdom, rather than reacting impulsively. By embracing mindful silence, we develop a deeper sense of inner peace and balance.

Moreover, mindful silence fosters a greater appreciation for the present moment. It encourages us to savor the simple pleasures of life and to find beauty in the ordinary. By integrating mindful silence into our daily routines, we enhance our overall well-being and enrich our experiences.

7

Chapter 7: Silence in the Workplace

The modern workplace is often characterized by constant noise and activity. However, incorporating moments of silence into our work environment can lead to increased productivity, creativity, and well-being.

Creating a quiet workspace allows us to minimize distractions and focus on our tasks. This can lead to improved concentration and efficiency, enabling us to accomplish more in less time. By prioritizing silence, we enhance our ability to perform at our best.

Moreover, silence can stimulate creativity and innovation. When we take breaks from constant stimulation, we give our minds the space to wander and explore new ideas. These periods of quiet reflection can lead to fresh insights and solutions.

In addition to its cognitive benefits, silence also promotes emotional well-being in the workplace. It provides an opportunity to decompress and recharge, reducing stress and preventing burnout. By incorporating moments of silence into our workday, we create a healthier and more balanced work environment.

Chapter 8: The Spiritual Dimension of Silence

Silence has long been recognized as a powerful tool for spiritual growth and connection. Many spiritual traditions emphasize the importance of quietude as a means of deepening our relationship with the divine and accessing higher states of consciousness.

Engaging in silent meditation or prayer allows us to transcend the noise of the external world and attune ourselves to the subtle energies within. This practice fosters a sense of inner peace and harmony, enabling us to connect with our higher selves and the divine.

Moreover, silence provides a space for spiritual reflection and contemplation. It allows us to explore our beliefs, values, and purpose, leading to greater spiritual clarity and understanding. By embracing silence, we create an environment conducive to spiritual growth and enlightenment.

Ultimately, silence is a gateway to spiritual awakening. It is in these quiet moments that we can experience a profound sense of connection with the universe and the divine. By harnessing the power of silence, we embark on a journey of spiritual discovery and transformation.

9

Chapter 9: Cultivating Silence in Daily Life

Incorporating moments of silence into our daily routines can have a profound impact on our overall well-being. By intentionally creating spaces for quietude, we can cultivate a sense of peace and balance in our lives.

One simple way to cultivate silence is by setting aside time each day for quiet reflection. This can be as brief as a few minutes of silent meditation or as long as an hour of solitude. These moments of silence provide an opportunity to unwind and reconnect with ourselves.

Additionally, we can create silent spaces in our homes and workplaces. Designating a quiet room or corner where we can retreat and recharge can make a significant difference in our well-being. By prioritizing silence, we create an environment that supports our mental and emotional health.

Furthermore, incorporating silent activities into our daily routines can enhance our overall well-being. Activities such as reading, journaling, or taking a quiet walk allow us to engage in silence and experience its benefits. By integrating silence into our lives, we foster a greater sense of peace and balance.

10

Chapter 10: Overcoming the Fear of Silence

For many people, silence can be uncomfortable, even frightening. The absence of noise and distraction forces us to confront our thoughts and emotions, which can be a daunting experience. However, overcoming the fear of silence is essential for harnessing its power and reaping its benefits.

One way to overcome this fear is by gradually introducing moments of silence into our daily routine. Start with just a few minutes of quiet time each day, gradually increasing the duration as you become more comfortable. This slow and steady approach allows you to build a tolerance for silence and develop a deeper appreciation for its benefits.

Additionally, it's important to recognize that silence is not synonymous with loneliness. Embracing silence can actually enhance our sense of connection with ourselves and others. By allowing ourselves to be present in the moment, we can develop a greater understanding of our emotions and cultivate a deeper sense of self-compassion.

Ultimately, overcoming the fear of silence requires a shift in perspective. Rather than viewing silence as something to be avoided, we can embrace it as a powerful tool for personal growth and transformation. By facing our fears and welcoming silence into our lives, we open ourselves up to a world of possibilities and inner peace.

11

Chapter 11: Silence as a Catalyst for Creativity

Silence is a powerful catalyst for creativity. When we create space for quietude, we allow our minds to wander freely and explore new ideas. In these moments of silence, we can tap into our creative potential and unleash our imagination.

One of the ways silence fosters creativity is by providing a break from constant stimulation. In our noisy world, we are often bombarded with information and distractions, leaving little room for creative thinking. Silence offers a respite from this chaos, allowing our minds to rest and rejuvenate.

Moreover, silence encourages us to engage in introspection and self-reflection. By turning our attention inward, we can explore our thoughts and emotions, leading to new insights and creative breakthroughs. In the quiet, we can connect with our inner muse and find inspiration in unexpected places.

Embracing silence as a catalyst for creativity requires a commitment to carving out quiet time in our daily lives. Whether it's through meditation, journaling, or simply sitting in silence, these moments of quietude can unlock our creative potential and lead to greater innovation and self-expression.

12

Chapter 12: Embracing Silence for a Balanced Life

Incorporating silence into our lives is essential for achieving a sense of balance and well-being. By intentionally creating moments of quietude, we can cultivate inner peace, enhance our relationships, and foster personal growth.

One of the key benefits of silence is its ability to promote mental and emotional clarity. In the absence of noise and distraction, we can process our thoughts and emotions more effectively, leading to greater self-awareness and emotional stability. This clarity allows us to make more informed decisions and navigate life's challenges with greater ease.

Moreover, silence enhances the quality of our interactions with others. By creating space for active listening and thoughtful communication, we can build deeper connections and foster a sense of trust and intimacy. Silence allows us to be fully present in our relationships, enriching our social and emotional bonds.

13

Chapter 13: Silence in Cultural Traditions

Silence holds a unique place in various cultural traditions around the world. Many societies recognize the profound impact of quietude on the human spirit and incorporate practices of silence into their rituals and daily lives.

In Eastern traditions, such as Buddhism and Taoism, silence is often seen as a pathway to enlightenment. Meditation practices, which emphasize silence and stillness, are central to these traditions. By quieting the mind, practitioners can achieve a state of inner peace and spiritual insight.

Indigenous cultures also place a high value on silence. For many Native American tribes, silence is a form of respect and a way to connect with the natural world. It is believed that through silence, one can listen to the wisdom of the earth and the ancestors.

In Western traditions, silence has been associated with contemplation and reflection. Monastic practices, such as those found in Christianity, often involve periods of silence for prayer and meditation. These practices allow individuals to deepen their connection with the divine and gain spiritual clarity.

14

Chapter 14: The Healing Power of Silence

Silence has remarkable healing properties, both physically and emotionally. It provides a sanctuary for the mind and body to recover and regenerate, promoting overall well-being.

Physically, silence can have a profound effect on our health. Research has shown that quiet environments can lower blood pressure, reduce heart rate, and boost the immune system. Silence also facilitates deeper, more restful sleep, which is essential for physical recovery and vitality.

Emotionally, silence provides a space for processing and healing. It allows us to confront and understand our emotions without the distractions of everyday life. In these quiet moments, we can gain clarity and perspective, leading to emotional resilience and well-being.

Moreover, silence can be a powerful tool for coping with grief and loss. It offers a space for reflection and remembrance, allowing us to honor our feelings and the memories of those we've lost. Through silence, we can find solace and healing in times of sorrow.

15

Chapter 15: Silence and Mental Clarity

In a world filled with constant noise and information overload, finding mental clarity can be challenging. However, silence offers a solution by providing a respite for our overworked minds.

By creating moments of silence, we give our brains the opportunity to reset and recharge. This mental break allows us to clear away the clutter and focus on what truly matters. In silence, we can prioritize our thoughts and gain a deeper understanding of our goals and aspirations.

Additionally, silence enhances our ability to concentrate and solve problems. Without the constant barrage of distractions, we can engage in deep, focused thinking. This clarity of mind leads to greater productivity and efficiency in both our personal and professional lives.

Ultimately, silence is essential for maintaining mental clarity and well-being. By incorporating periods of quiet into our daily routines, we can achieve a greater sense of focus and direction. This mental clarity empowers us to navigate life's challenges with confidence and purpose.

16

Chapter 16: Creating a Personal Silence Sanctuary

Incorporating silence into our lives can be challenging, especially in noisy and chaotic environments. However, by creating a personal silence sanctuary, we can carve out a space for quietude and reflection.

A silence sanctuary can be any space that offers a respite from noise and distractions. This could be a quiet room in your home, a secluded spot in a park, or even a cozy corner with a comfortable chair and soothing decor. The key is to design a space that feels peaceful and inviting.

In your silence sanctuary, you can engage in various activities that promote quietude and mindfulness. This could include meditation, journaling, reading, or simply sitting in silence and observing your surroundings. These practices help you connect with the present moment and cultivate a sense of inner peace.

Creating a personal silence sanctuary is an investment in your well-being. It provides a dedicated space for relaxation, reflection, and personal growth. By prioritizing silence in your life, you can create a haven of tranquility amidst the chaos of the world.

Chapter 17: Silence and the Art of Listening

Listening is an essential skill that is often overlooked in our fast-paced, noisy world. However, silence is a key component of effective listening, allowing us to truly hear and understand others.

When we embrace silence in our conversations, we create space for others to express themselves fully. This active listening fosters deeper connections and empathy, as we can truly understand the perspectives and emotions of those we engage with.

Moreover, silence allows us to listen to the unspoken. By paying attention to body language, facial expressions, and other non-verbal cues, we can gain a deeper understanding of the underlying emotions and intentions of others. This heightened awareness enhances our communication skills and strengthens our relationships.

Ultimately, silence is a powerful tool for cultivating the art of listening. By embracing quiet moments in our interactions, we can foster more meaningful and authentic connections with others. Listening with an open heart and mind allows us to build trust, understanding, and harmony in our relationships.

Book Description

CHAPTER 17: SILENCE AND THE ART OF LISTENING

"Empowered Silence: Harnessing the Power of Quietude" explores the transformative potential of silence and offers practical guidance on how to integrate it into our lives. Through twelve chapters, we have delved into the essence of silence, its scientific and emotional benefits, and its profound impact on our relationships, work, and spiritual journey. We have learned that silence is not merely the absence of noise but a powerful state filled with potential for creativity, emotional stability, and personal growth.

By overcoming the fear of silence and embracing its benefits, we can unlock a deeper connection with ourselves and the world around us. Whether it's through mindful silence, spending time in nature, or creating quiet spaces in our daily lives, we can harness the power of silence to achieve a more balanced and fulfilling life. Ultimately, silence is a gateway to self-discovery, inner peace, and personal transformation. By integrating moments of quietude into our routines, we can cultivate a sense of calm and clarity, leading to a richer and more meaningful existence.

www.ingramcontent.com/pod-product-compliance
Lightning Source LLC
LaVergne TN
LVHW010446070526
838199LV00066B/6221